Beautiful Artifacts

Beautiful Artifacts

Poems by

Stork Rein

© 2024 Stork Rein. All rights reserved.
This material may not be reproduced in any form, published,
reprinted, recorded, performed, broadcast,
rewritten, or redistributed without
the explicit permission of Stork Rein.
All such actions are strictly prohibited by law.

Cover design by Shay Culligan
Cover image by Darlene Frascone
Author photo by Erika Rein

ISBN: 978-1-63980-656-0
Library of Congress Control Number: 2024946845

Kelsay Books
502 South 1040 East, A-119
American Fork, Utah 84003
Kelsaybooks.com

For Erika, for everything

Acknowledgments

Thank you to the following publications, in which versions of these poems previously appeared:

The Citadel: "Breath"
Mono Magazine: "Returning to the Cauldron"
Remington Review: "Dreaming of Whitman"

Contents

I

daughter	15
Drowning, in winter	16
After the Flood	17
Collections	18
Sketches	20
Machu Picchu	21
Pentimento	23
love, three haikus	25
On the Last Page of the Classified Ads	26
Broken	27
Dreaming of Whitman	29
Returning to the Cauldron	30
Snake	31
Fenceline	33
Beyond the Edge of Getting	35

II

God, Noah, and the Eastern Seaboard	39
Lava	40
Blue	42
November Fifth	43
Breath	44
Startled Fish	46
Shai'hulud	47
Toward a Gentle Rising	48
Take This Waltz	49
Pareidolia	50
What Comes Next	51

"She stood beside me for years, or was it a moment?
I cannot remember. Maybe I loved her, maybe I didn't.
There was a house, and then no house. There were trees,
but none remain. You, whose moments are gone,
who drift like smoke in the afterlife, tell me
something, tell me anything."

—Mark Strand

I

daughter

dried leaves blowing free
the wind in failing sunlight
sorrow fills the air

Drowning, in winter

I stop counting
the skips every time
I think of you.
I wait until the full
moon to travel, scared
to trace the scent
of emptiness in broad
daylight, where unseen
sparks can catch me on fire.

Your clothes have lost
their aroma—flowers
and musk—hang sad
on their hangers.

When I finally
gather up your items
for the trash bin,
I notice that your favorite
suitcase is missing,
and your fine black shoes.

After the Flood

On the door it says what to do to survive
But we were not born to survive
Only to live
                —W.S. Merwin

I arise. Dreams coil and dissipate around my feet.
A giant oak stands watch over the entrance to a sheltered
glade. I have been brought here before,
but much has changed.

The meadow, whose soil once churned under
the horses of grief, lies still under a fresh layer of snow.
Trees drip quietly upon the earth.
The sky is radiant with morning light.

A stream that overflowed its banks with white
bone and dark water moves on, subterranean, at peace
with gravity once again. And it comes to me—
that our constructed calendars

are artificial comfort, designed as circular,
so that we can revisit dates and times, mark events
as important, or tragic. But time is not
circular, it spirals forward towards

some unknowable conclusion.
Sadness a sudden companion.
A flock of blackbirds against the sun,
cinders tossed onto white snow.

Collections

*Sunlights differ
but there is only one night.*
   —Ursula K. LeGuin

Going through collections
of now, of then,
my CDs stand on the wall
with the one you left
in that funky player in my old car,
musical evidence
of father-daughter bonding.

Did you leave it for me to find later?
Don't know.
I know that you liked it—
James, The Best Of.
With no cover no label
no explanation
it was shuffled, buried and
shifted around before joining
the assortment of music in the
enclosed case at our home.

It's been fifteen years
or fifteen days
or hours
since you slipped away
from that too bright space
into irrevocable darkness.
Do I think of you often?
No.
Do I miss you terribly?
All of the time.

I start James in the Marantz player
crank up the amp
curl on the floor next to you,
the best of us weaving through
the notes of violin and guitar.
I reach for your imaginary hand.

Sketches

unfair battle
scrub jay vs. finch
finch song wins

election day: 11/8/16
leonard cohen's death: 11/7/16
the wisdom of that man

sun shaft dust motes
green stockings by the nightstand
early 20's morning

I asked her about her father's .45
she patted the bed and smiled
then turned out the light

mifepristone pills
controlled by small-handed cops
the devil has the claws of a man

wild cakebread and stag's leap vines
creep across cracked floors
crows and seagulls wheel in semaphores

at the end on the boat's last sailing
shall we balance life's ledger
or just open our mouths and sing?

Machu Picchu

after Sara Littlecrow-Russell

I heard you before I saw you.

Downstream from the Inca ruins
in the high grass
you were quoting
Luis Javier Rodriguez
to the various animals
who were your only audience.

When I found you
I turned speechless,
not daring to break
that ephemeral moment
of light wind, deerskin,
your enchanting voice.

We walked together.
When I finally tried
to speak, you put your
finger to my lips,
which still burn from
that touch.

You taught me how to hunt,
to fish, to build a fire
with only our hands
and offerings from nature.

That night
we rubbed our tattoos together,
I—the fox,
you—the owl,
sparks flying up and through the ceiling.

In the morning,
I was covered with feathers.
You had gone to follow the sun.

I will find you.
I can fly now.

Pentimento

It is sometime in July.
The variegated hum of flying insects
rises and falls
as they swing close and move away
from the front porch where I sit
sipping tea, watching clusters
of people picking blackberries across the street.
They arrive in pickup trucks,
SUVs and tiny Hondas,
cruising by, backing up,
maneuvering to the best spots.
The experienced pickers come prepared
with buckets and bags
and sometimes, ladders.
I smile at their enthusiasm for braving
the thorns that guard the sweet fruit.

A green leaf of memory unfurls
from a grey space in my chest:
picking berries
next to the old water tower, with her.
The black and red succulence,
the pleasure—a prelude
to the passion later in our marriage bed.
I turn to remind her, to reminisce,
but she's not there, her teacup empty.
Dust in her cup.
Dust in my head.

"Dad, you need to write these things down!"
A past admonishment from my son,
who happens to be picking berries
across the street
with my grandson, Hank.

He meant my appointments,
taking my meds,
picking up dry cleaning.
But the important things,
events cleaved from the past,
not the future,
are not to be so mastered.
They come unbidden,
leaving another layer
of suffering when they depart.

Two tiger swallowtails sweep down
from the edge of the roof, juke and jink
around the garden, kiss the roses
and black-eyed Susans,
then lose themselves behind the lavender bush.

love, three haikus

she tills the garden
I survey her fertile lines
we seed together

moonlight on her curves
startles my dream to longing
for a morning kiss

I knew her not well
until I washed and folded
her soft underwear

On the Last Page of the Classified Ads

I'm a carver
with a complete set of tools.
I have the hands of God,
should God be a woman.
Give me your unfinished pieces
of youth, time, and memories,
any words shuttered by fear.

I will carve away all
that you do not want to see,
touch, or remember,
and leave you
with a beautiful artifact.

Do not pay me.
I will cup my hands and hold
what is left on the carving room floor
as the real treasure,
not what you carry away.

Broken

I stand across from my childhood home
under a streetlamp's sallow light,

clenching and unclenching the handle
of the knife pocketed in my winter coat.

Snow on the ground, a mist of rain.
A few leaves on skeletons of trees

agitate in the wind, soon to succumb
to shear vectors and gravity.

I bend old memories into words that drop
into my hands, wring as much truth

from them as I can, examine the bones
that remain. His bones are my bones.

My father shuffles like a shadow between rooms
in the house, now fronted by a dilapidated

porch and a screen door that hangs listlessly
from one hinge. There's only one shadow now—

my mother left the only man
she would call husband ten years ago,

worn down by the broken things in her marriage—
washing machine, toilet, weed-infested

yard, a love crushed by his anger. They met
under the ochre arch next to her high school.

She was so young. He was so married.
She never stood a chance.

Self-emancipated years later,
she escaped to a small sunlit apartment

that was a joy to visit. We cooked meals together.
I read her poetry. Everything worked.

Now, I wait until the lights begin to turn off—
first in the living room stuffed with boxes

of old magazines and a TV with a cracked
screen, then in the unused kitchen, a hotel

for mice, and then the bathroom, until only
the bedroom's dim bulb is lit. The hunched

figure of my father slouches on the edge
of an unmade bed, then slowly lies down.

I step back and away, up the tilted porch steps
to the front door, pull the knife from my pocket.

His heart is not my heart.
He can swallow me no longer.

I return the abandoned hinge at the bottom
to its rightful place and use the knife to tighten

in the four screws, then fix the four at the top
until the fit is right, and the door hangs true.

Dreaming of Whitman

I sit beneath the aged oak
to slake my need for shade
and rough bark behind my back.
Gazing at miraculous grass
and drawing life from fragrant air,
I become aware
that rain has started falling
through star-shaped leaves
and down.

It does not stop
upon touching ground,
but sinks to roots,
draws upwards
to shoots
of lush greenery,
and last to acorns that soon
will drop to fertile soil.

At a distance I sense
the City's engine sputter and start,
the beckoning, churning sound
of ten thousand dusty feet shuffling
towards a hundred corporate gates.

But I turn away
from that familiar, seductive call
towards this different voice.

I will sit beneath the ancient oak,
caress the grassy felt,
listen to this song—the all
that is myself, dreaming of Whitman.

Returning to the Cauldron

Aged wood relaxes into ignition, reaches down to foster kindling,
foretelling that this is how it will always be,
every maple tree dies a little death with each leaf falling.

I lean over my cane toward warmth, the untamed forest
of my youth behind me, surrounded by other footprints
in the dirt and sand, the fire's grand cauldron calling.

The face of my father is missing from the flames,
but I no longer blame myself for that or any of his crooked paths.
An unlit torch is a torch that cannot be passed.

I wonder what life and home were like in his years before
he fell into other women's arms, his superficial charms fading
as he tossed apple after half-eaten apple into the cooling ash.

My son now has a son, my work is nearly done, at least
until after the next long sleep. I pray that I taught him enough,
loved him enough, held him enough, to keep his own love aloft.

The ocean rises and roars. This cauldron simmered
long before this night, still I peer over the rim, dip in
my tempered fingers, examine pieces too hardened, or too soft.

Snake

My older half-brother, Carl,
killed snakes for pleasure.
He would get everyone's attention
whenever we barbecued in his
back yard, point out a snake
resting in the cool grass, and say,
There's a rattler, gonna get him!
Betty, his girlfriend, stood by,
chain smoking, her eyes offering
mute encouragement.

Carl would grab a shovel and
with a quick downward chop
slice through the snake's body
just below the head, then raise
its remaining tail, still wriggling,
over his head in triumph,
as if he were Perseus hoisting
the severed head of Medusa.
But it never was a rattler—
it was a garter snake,
innocent, beautifully striped,
dry-glistening in the sun.

Carl died before he was 60
from a terminal combination
of diabetes and alcoholism.
He was buried in a cemetery
a stone's throw from his house.

I often wonder if all
those severed snake tails
sensed him, if they wriggled
underground to where he lay
and whipped him
until he begged for forgiveness.

Fenceline

As a boy, I stood
by a pond, skipping
stones next to god—
spinning slaps
slowed by viscous
water until the final
plop. Scrawny tanned
legs, the air suspended
on summer.

On a zig-zag trail
by a horse farm,
I met M. Scott Peck
dragged along by
an old bulldog.
I asked
   why did you say nothing
   about the endless number of roads
he said
   tell me what you are looking for
I answered
   small flat stones and a body of water
he shook his head
   you are traveling alongside the fence
   jump over
then continued down the path,
the bulldog following behind.

72 winters.
A train's mortal cry
echoes in the frosted hills,
a lone jay
squawks at the falling snow.

The almost-white patterns of
my empty dinner plate.

The wind bows to wise stones,
wreathed in moss,
that lie beneath the frozen lake.

Beyond the Edge of Getting

in the blaze of promise
everywhere
the eyes of morning
edged with rain fall on
every word that is written

I gaze at a tree's baby green buds
confused by this too long winter
steam rises from the ashen cedar fence
a laundry line sags under the watch
of prayer flags in stilled contemplation

Jan Garbarek's tenor sax sings
from the gramophone
flows across the grey lit room
the spartan writing table the
inked quill poised to write something

to write anything
waiting for the music to unlock lines
open the doors of heaven
reveal angels in the shape of flies
that are still artifacts of glory

II

God, Noah, and the Eastern Seaboard

Spun by the hurricane,
the broken terra cotta vase
lies on the bed that was
deserted as a haven for the two
who were once one,
the house now empty
after the dark green shadows
arrived like an early warning system.

Mattress, couch, chairs soaked,
standing water in half of the rooms,
windows and picture glass shattered.

The waters shall never again become a flood?

Tell that to the two
terra cotta lovers
whose one-mass embrace
was torn asunder.

Lava

I watch long legged spiders
weave gossamer silk
with their forelegs
in the corner of a Cotati
kitchen window.
Outside, a towering
bamboo grove
shifts and clatters
in the southern garden.

I am struck by sun
and shade that call
for attention, but my mind
wanders north
to fire and smoke
threatening our home,
our neighbors' homes,
the foundations of our lives.

I am no longer a young
man. I feel the cold breath
waiting at the end of the road.
How fast could I run,
if I needed to?
I'm running now, just sitting still.

Forty-foot black
skeletons of trees
line both sides of Interstate 5
as we return home to Mount Shasta.

They stand in mute agony,
giant stick figures caught
by a sweeping incendiary
flash that left only their
shadows behind,
across miles and miles
of the Delta Fire aftermath.
Thousands of shadows.
Hundreds of ghosts.

Children coughing through nights
of choking dust, hiding,
scrabbling for food and water.
Shelter just a rumor.
Millions of ghosts.
Most will say they knew her.
The sound of water dripping into a ruined future.

Blue

I'm standing by her bed, watching her sleep as only young
children can, in open mouth abandon. It is an hour

before dawn, the house so quiet that I can hear it sigh and
shift on its bones. I share its sadness, its uncertainty,

knowing that soon I will walk out its front door for the last time.
I lay my hand on top of her head, that soft hair.

I tell her that I'm sorry, that one day she will understand, that
I will see her again, despite the great distance that will exist

between us. She does not stir. I cross to the window facing
the west yard, the lawn painted in a coat of full moon.

Far away, across the great ravine, a village faintly appears
in the deep blue hills, amber lighted windows suggesting small

homes, small mercies. My destination—unknown, enthralling.
She whispers dreamspeak in her bed. The moon begins to pale,

a nod towards sunrise. Robins begin their waking songs.
Below the window, a dead fox lies cooling in the silver grass.

November Fifth

Wounded garden
spilt seed
split pods
my cracks, showing.

No amount of water
no amount of uncaring sun
will ever cause any buried shoots to arise.
And what would I say should that happen?

how you have grown.
how old are the twins now?
do you still drink yourself to sleep each night?
do you forgive my trespasses?

I'm still working on yours.

Breath

I try to find space
to breathe
in between the beeps
and the blinking
of a darkened room in the ICU.
I hold her hand, limp
as the rest of her, thinking that
I watched her being born
in a room very similar to this.
What terrible symmetry
this night has visited upon the two of us.

A doctor and a nurse arrive,
check the intubation tube
and the beeping and the blinking,
consult with each other, then me.
Liver and kidneys failing, internal
bleeding, her BP keeps dropping,
the drugs they have pumped into her
for a week have now reached
their limits of effectiveness.
"She is not a good candidate for a transplant."
There is a long pause. I nod, hearing
what they're not saying, not asking,
a decision to be made.
The light on their faces
is not the light on my face.

They leave.

A quiet chorus of conversation
drifts in through the open door
from a farther room, a dozen
friends and family waiting for a word
of their fallen angel, the flawed father.

She and I had almost reached
a point of understanding.
She, accepting that I had to leave.
I, realizing that I never
should have left her behind.
It was an absence that became so toxic
that it turned combustible,
then caught fire and burned
everything on the perimeter
before turning inward
to finish its work.

I kiss the hand that I am holding,
breathing, breaking.

I wake, the waking stumbles me
to the familiar toothbrush, shower, shave.
The walls keep me from falling down.
I wish I could forget all of this
like forgetting to turn the burner off,
or return a book to a friend.
I wish my heart had wings.
I wish the sky weren't so blue.
Walking November's frost-blasted garden
I search for the makings of soup.
Thyme, rosemary, a few smooth stones.

Startled Fish

The ocean wind
and you and I sculpt miniature
sand figures at the waterline.
I pick up pebbles
and put them in a plastic bucket,
babbling about
how shiny they are.
Look—those are stones
that were her eyes! Only then do

I see the evening tide
ghosting your sandprints
trailing along the shore.
I can't catch up to where they end—
their beginnings, strangely,
are easier to recall.

You never loved anything
so much as the moment
it was gone. Fleeing
like a school of startled fish,
you bathed in the melancholy
of separation, only to come back
later, weeds pushing up
through concrete.
What faint star did you
navigate by, what was your
sustenance, who did you feed on?

Brown pelicans lift and fall in flight.
From a great distance, Famadihana
music begins to move upon the waters.

Shai'hulud

It is said that God created
the desert to train the faithful.

I lost my faith when I lost my child.

When a stranger smiled, I felt strange.
When a singer sang, I lost my voice.
In a crowded room, I felt alone.

I walked into the desert
until I could walk no more.
There was sand beneath my knees.

Shai'hulud.
Roc ravens.
Spiked creature
that is my soul:
May the wind sear my shame.
May the dunes shelter my heart.
May I walk tall through the sirocco,
my head a mile from the earth,
where sin falls away
as it empties into the face of God.

Toward a Gentle Rising

riders garbed in yellow-green
hover over their electric bikes

a woman in a hajib and head-to-toe black
breaks bread with a biker and sun-eyed

grackles   dogs everywhere   no one bites
or snaps or uses harsh language   all talk as if

between lifelong friends but we know
otherwise by how shyly they say hello

each connected to a watery emergence
that began a half billion years ago

somewhere in the breezeway the sound
of a piano's tinkling keys drifts across

the vegetables and fruits of the
Toby's Feed Barn farmers market

light   gentle   as easy as the visitors
who stroll past with bagels and coffee

the hole in the center of a bagel formed
to release steam during final baking

creates color that brings sweetness
or at least toward an idea of sweetness

such an easy thing to do   such a simple
thought to offer   to share openings

Take This Waltz

The black oak with the beautiful scars
said, come—it is time to dance.
The sunflowers nodded,
seeds fell,
hummingbirds hummed.

The black dog said, no—
these are the days of August,
there is no time to waste—
dig with me, lay down with me,
gnaw these bones for burial.

What used to rise as important
no longer arises.
All of my corners have been
sanded smooth, reaching
toward a perfect circle. Simple.

Jane H. was right—I will have to choose.

It was getting on dusk before I could
waltz and glide around the patient tree.
The bones lay in the cooling grass,
the breeze swirled like a summer dress.
We let the sleeping dog lie.

Pareidolia

*the tendency to perceive a specific and often meaningful
image in a random or ambiguous pattern.*

I stare
at the melting rivulets of butter
on my toasted bagel.
I realize
that I must be looking for a sign,
or a message.

The sign is:
   time for another bagel.
The message is:
   your life is not butter, easily melted
   and neither is it toast.
   It was never burned
   as badly as you thought
   and, yes—those could be wings
   on your back, if you would
   only learn how to unfold.

What Comes Next

My breath charges the chilling air
as I watch the sun
set and flow into
the dark hills of the future.
My youth has come full circle,
I find myself coming up behind
my other self, soft grape greeting
raisin wrapped in its wrinkled wisdom.
We will sit, then, good company always,
comfortable in the atmosphere
as it thickens and shapes the air,
searching for the seams between
this world and the next.

About the Author

Stork Rein had the fortune of being taught by an innovative high school English teacher who brought *The Waste Land* to class for reading and analysis. His poetry neurons began firing then and have yet to be stilled. His work has appeared in *The Ekphrastic Review, Mono Magazine, Remington Review,* and *The Citadel.*

Stork lives in the alpine community of Mount Shasta, California with his wife Erika.

He can be reached at:
stork@storkreinpoetry.com

www.ingramcontent.com/pod-product-compliance
Lightning Source LLC
Chambersburg PA
CBHW030916170426
43193CB00009BA/880